Evil English Castles

Nasty Deeds and Skulduggery

Designed by Melvin Creative

Printed in China

Published by

GW Publishing
PO Box 15070,
Dunblane,
FK15 5AN

www.gwpublishing.com

ISBN 978-0-9570844-5-2

CONTENTS

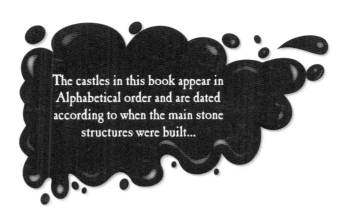

The castles in this book appear in Alphabetical order and are dated according to when the main stone structures were built...

TYPES OF CASTLES

CASTLES WERE BUILT IN MANY DIFFERENT SHAPES AND SIZES THROUGHOUT ENGLAND. HERE ARE SOME OF THE MAIN TYPES.

Motte and Bailey

These timber castles were built by the Normans from 1066. The Motte could be a natural hill, but was usually man-made, using earth and layers of stones. The Bailey was a walled enclosure, protecting the soldiers and their livestock.

KEEP

MOTTE

PALISADE

MOAT

BAILEY

DRAWBRIDGE

Square Stone Keep

These stone castles were built to last, with thick walls which would rise above all other buildings. Rochester Castle (page 48) standing at 34.5 metres (113 ft), is the highest stone keep castle in England. Some Keeps were built with the front door on the first floor, and with removable stairs leading up to the entrance, in case the castle was attacked.

Stone Shell Keep

Stone shell keeps became popular in the early twelfth century, replacing the timber Keeps on a Motte. They were designed to surround and protect the stone or timber buildings within them. See Clifford's Tower on page 22.

INNER WARD

INNER WALL

OUTER WARD

OUTER CURTAIN WALL

Concentric Castle

These castles had two surrounding walls with towers along them. The inner wall was higher than the outer wall. King Edward I built many of these in Wales, in the late thirteenth century.

INTRODUCTION

Defences and strongholds have been built in England since the earliest times. Many of them were built by the Romans almost 2,000 years ago. A few castles were built about fifteen years before the Norman invasion in 1066, but when the Normans (French) arrived, led by William the Duke of Normandy, castles began to be built on a vast scale, all over England.

William had brought about 10,000 men with him, making it difficult for the Saxons to fight them off and to protect themselves. As William's army spread across the country, so more and more Norman fortresses were built. The Saxon population didn't want the Normans there, but all the big showy castles made sure they knew who was in charge.

These castles were mainly timber Motte (earth mound) and Bailey (defensive courtyard) castles, which could be built very quickly as long as there was a forest nearby and plenty of shovels. The castles were built in strategic places, very often on the sites of old Roman forts.

There were hundreds of these castles all over England, but being made of wood they were vulnerable to being set on fire and destroyed. So, they were eventually replaced by stone.

The original timber castles have disappeared, but some of the Mottes can still be seen up and down the country, and many of the stone castles are as frightening and grand as ever.

This book is about some of these great stone castles.

Some became lovely palaces; some were fearsome fortresses.

Some were used as gruesome prisons; and many were used for *all* of these purposes.

So let's find out what castles were all about!

William the Conqueror

When Edward the Confessor died childless in 1066, there were several claims to the English throne. Edward's brother-in-law, Harold Godwinson, was crowned immediately but William, Duke of Normandy, said that Edward had promised the throne to him, so he decided to come and take the crown from Harold.

The Norman Invasion

On the 28th September William's flagship 'The Mora' and a fleet of about **800 ships** landed at Pevensey on the Sussex coast. With King Harold and his army busy fighting the Vikings in York, William's invasion force of about 7,000 to 10,000 men didn't have to fight when coming ashore. (Which was nice for them!)

The first thing William the Conqueror did was establish a base at Pevensey. There was already an old Roman shore fort there which had been taken over by the Saxons so it was the obvious place. William had a temporary motte and bailey timber castle quickly constructed within the walls of the fort which stood until it was replaced with a majestic stone castle. The new castle was besieged four times, but was never captured by force. It was surrendered twice however, through lack of food.

WILLIAM THE CONQUEROR

Edward promised I could be the King of England!

Grrr

..Rarrr

Blaaa

Na-Na Ni-Na-Na

First the Vikings, now the NORMANS!!! Can you come back next week?

The Battle of Hastings

When the Normans met King Harold and his army 10 miles along the coast at Hastings on the 14th October, Harold's men were positioned on a hill. This was making things a bit difficult for the Normans, but William had a tactic that he had used before. William's army pretended to run away, so Harold's men came running down the hill chasing them. William's army with experienced knights turned around and attacked from sides, killing Harold and defeating his army.

After the battle, William worked his way around London, taking Dover, Canterbury, Winchester, Newbury and finally Berkhamsted where he met a delegation from London who, in surrendering, offered William the crown. He said he would accept the keys to London in Berkhamsted, but demanded that he should be crowned in London. So William became King of England on Christmas Day, 1066.....in London!

The Normans brought with them a few ready to assemble castles along with skilled Carpenters. Over 500 Motte and Bailey timber castles (see page 4) would be built across England in the years that followed. These castles gave the Normans secure bases for their men and horses in a hostile country and also show the Saxons that King William was in charge.

Some of the finest castles in this book that were started by William the Conqueror are:

Corfe, Dover, Lincoln, Rochester, Warwick, Windsor, and the White Tower (of London).

KING HAROLD

Don't Worry Men! I've still got one good eye!! NOW...point me in the right direction.

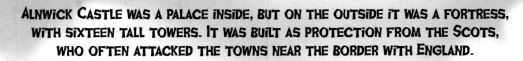

ALNWICK CASTLE WAS A PALACE INSIDE, BUT ON THE OUTSIDE IT WAS A FORTRESS, WITH SIXTEEN TALL TOWERS. IT WAS BUILT AS PROTECTION FROM THE SCOTS, WHO OFTEN ATTACKED THE TOWNS NEAR THE BORDER WITH ENGLAND.

A Siege Trick

In 1093, King Malcolm III of Scotland attacked the castle. The defenders said they would only surrender if Malcolm received the keys of the castle.

So a knight rode out from the castle with the keys dangling on the end of his spear.

King Malcolm rode forward to accept them, but the devious knight pierced Malcolm with the spear, killing him and leaving his men without anyone to give them instructions on how to fight.

This set the Scots into a panic, and the defenders rushed quickly from the castle and defeated them.

So, remember ... NEVER trust a knight dangling keys on a spear!

Alnwick Castle

That fella's bringing oot the keys on a stick for ye!

He seems like a nice man!

He's a very nice man!

A great guy!

Well I smell a RAT!

HEY

Three cheers for the very nice man!

ALNWICK CASTLE 1096 (PRONOUNCED: ANNICK)

THE NORMANS BUILT A MOTTE AND BAILEY CASTLE HERE, IN 1096 THEN, IN 1309, THE POWERFUL PERCY FAMILY BOUGHT IT AND MADE HUGE CHANGES. ALNWICK IS NOW THE SECOND LARGEST INHABITED CASTLE IN ENGLAND, AFTER WINDSOR CASTLE.

In 1172, it was besieged by King William of Scotland.

He failed to take the castle, but had another try in 1174.

He probably wished he had learned his lesson the first time, when he was captured by 400 English Knights.

The Scots never gave up though, and attacked it again and again over the following 100 years.

The HUNCHBACKED VAMPIRE

People have reported seeing a tall, hunchbacked vampire. It is said that a former Lord lived underground, and only came out at night to attack villagers.

Terror-meter

THE CASTLE OVERLOOKS THE RIVER ARUN, IN WEST SUSSEX AND HAS BEEN THE FAMILY HOME OF THE DUKES OF NORFOLK FOR OVER 850 YEARS. DURING THE FIRST ENGLISH CIVIL WAR, IN 1642–1646, THE CASTLE WAS FOUGHT OVER BETWEEN THE ROUNDHEADS, WHO SUPPORTED PARLIAMENT, AND THE ROYALISTS, WHO SUPPORTED THE KING.

Grrrrr!

Hsssss!

ROUNDHEADS V CAVALIERS

The Roundheads were led by Oliver Cromwell and were against kings or queens having power over the country. They mostly had short hair and wore plain clothes. The Royalists, who were also known as "Cavaliers", wanted **King Charles 1** to have complete control. They usually had long curly hair and wore fancy clothes.

Down with the Royalists

Oliver Cromwell

They're just jealous because we're better looking!

King Charles 1

I'm Starving!

C'mon down... It's Christmas! We're having custard for afters!

A Christmas Siege

The Roundheads captured the castle in 1642, but the Royalists took it back again in 1643! The Roundheads were determined to get the castle back again, so they returned in December, with **5,000 men**, and laid siege. The 800 men defending the castle had stored most of their food in the town. So, all the Roundheads had to do was wait!

By Christmas, the Royalists were starving and the Roundheads were not going to give them **Christmas Dinner**, or send them presents! The Royalists finally surrendered on 6th January, 1644. By the end of the Civil War the castle was in ruins, and was not rebuilt for almost 100 years.

from the Roundheads

ARUNDEL CASTLE 1138

THE STONE SHELL KEEP OF THE CASTLE WAS BUILT IN 1138. IT STANDS ON TOP OF THE MOTTE, WHICH WAS ONCE PART OF THE MOTTE AND BAILEY CASTLE ERECTED BY THE NORMANS IN 1068.

THE DARK SIDE

In the past, a small **white bird** has appeared fluttering around the windows. This has always been followed by the **death** of a castle resident.

The **ghost** of a young boy called the "Serving Lad" has been seen in the kitchen, washing pots and pans.

Since 1630, a **Blue Man** has been seen **floating** around the library reading the books.

Terror-meter

Bamburgh Castle

NO ROYALTY

KING WILLIAM II

Knock Knock

It was a joke! Of course I'm not going to poke out your eyes!

The castle came under siege after the rebel Earl, Robert De Mowbray, conspired to get rid of King William II, in 1095. The King built a huge tower near the castle, which he called Malveisin, which means "Evil Neighbour".

Mowbray escaped but was captured a week later. King William threatened to gouge out his eyes in front of everyone still in the castle, including his wife, so they agreed to give up.

BOOOOM

SMASH

In 1464, the castle, held by Sir Ralph Grey, came under siege by the Earl of Warwick. The Earl had brought five big cannons with him and sent Bamburgh in to history, making it the first castle in England to fall as a result of the use of gunpowder.

As the castle was being blasted apart, Ralph Grey was knocked out and buried under falling stones. The garrison surrendered and Sir Ralph, still suffering from his injuries, was tied to his horse and dragged to Doncaster. He was put on trial for treason and then beheaded.

CLUNK

Yaa-Owch!

This is a bit of a drag!

Arrrrrggggghhhhh

SIR RALPH GREY

What a day I've had! I really don't think it could get any worse!

MUM

Hee Hee Hee, Wanna bet? Shhhhhhh!

Cannons were given names, and the five that pounded Bamburgh were called: "Edward"; "Dijon"; "London"; "Newcastle"; and "Richard Bombartel".

BAMBURGH CASTLE 1164

CALLED "THE FOUNDATION STONE OF ENGLAND", MIGHTY BAMBURGH CASTLE SITS 50 METRES (165FT) ABOVE THE COAST OF NORTHUMBERLAND, IN NORTH-EAST ENGLAND. IT HAS ALWAYS BEEN A VERY IMPORTANT SITE, EVER SINCE NORTHUMBRIA BECAME THE MOST POWERFUL OF THE SEVEN KINGDOMS DURING THE DARK AGES ... BEFORE THE KINGDOM OF ENGLAND EVEN EXISTED.

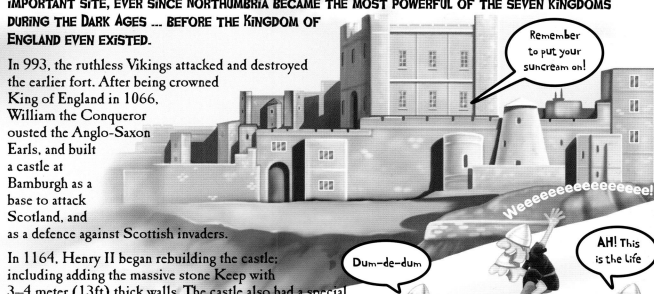

In 993, the ruthless Vikings attacked and destroyed the earlier fort. After being crowned King of England in 1066, William the Conqueror ousted the Anglo-Saxon Earls, and built a castle at Bamburgh as a base to attack Scotland, and as a defence against Scottish invaders.

In 1164, Henry II began rebuilding the castle; including adding the massive stone Keep with 3–4 meter (13ft) thick walls. The castle also had a special bottle-shaped doorway, so that soldiers could come in without getting off their horses.

Remember to put your suncream on!

Weeeeeeeeeeeeeeeeeee!

Dum-de-dum

AH! This is the life

The VIKINGS

HAHA! What a rubbish little castle. These Saxons must be TINY!

Crush Em!!!

Grrrrr!

The ghost, called "the Pink Lady", is said to appear every seven years. She wanders the castle then stands looking out to sea, searching for her lost lover.

Seven years I've been waiting here. No phone call, email, nothing!

Treasure Hunt

It has been said that King Richard II hid some of his personal treasure at Beeston Castle, before he was deposed by King Henry IV, in 1399.

Where has he hidden that treasure?

Where can it be?

He'll never find it!

King Richard II

Maybe here?

BEEP! BEEP!

Prumppp

Not there! YUK!

PONG!

Some people think that Richard threw his valuables into the well, which at 110 meters (370ft) deep is the deepest medieval well in England.

It is also thought that there may be hidden passageways near the bottom of the well.

Others say his treasure is buried somewhere in the castle grounds, but no one has been able to find it. Anyone want to buy a metal detector?

Find the Coins

Can you find 6 Gold coins hidden on these pages?

Nope!

If you find any.... they're mine!

King Henry IV

14

BEESTON CASTLE 1225

BEESTON WAS BUILT AROUND 1225, BY RANULF BLONDEVILLE, THE EARL OF CHESTER, AFTER HIS RETURN FROM THE FIFTH CRUSADE. IT SITS ON A HIGH, ROCKY PEAK, OVERLOOKING THE COUNTY OF CHESHIRE.

KNOWN AS "THE CASTLE ON THE ROCK", BEESTON WAS BUILT TO SHOW OFF, AND AS A DEFENSIVE FORTRESS, WITH MASSIVE WALLS, A HUGE GATEHOUSE, D-SHAPED TOWERS, CLIFFS ON THREE SIDES, AND A 9 METRE (30FT) DEEP DITCH TO THE FRONT.

During the English Civil War, in 1643, Beeston was held by a garrison of 300 Roundheads, led by a Captain Steele. On a December night, while the Captain slept, 9 Royalist soldiers crept into the castle and managed to open the gates for more soldiers to enter.

With the castle taken, the garrison was allowed to leave unharmed, but Captain Steele's commanders were not so kind and had him shot for not holding the castle.

In 1237, King Henry III further strengthened its defences during his battles with Wales, and used it to hold Welsh captives.

CAPTAIN STEELE

shhhh

zzzZZ

I knew we took the wrong turn back there!

WALES RU

Referee's a bit strict!

Take them to the dungeon!

The castle was partially destroyed by Cromwell's Roundheads in 1646.

OOPS!

The Crusades were attempts by the Catholic Church to take control of the Holy Lands. 'Crusade' is french for 'taking up the cross'.

SIR KNOW-A-LOT

Terror-meter

ALMOST EVERY CASTLE IN ENGLAND HAS COME UNDER ATTACK AT SOME TIME, BUT THE DEFENCES OF BODIAM WERE NEVER TESTED IN A SIEGE. SURROUNDED BY A WIDE MOAT, THE LIVING CHAMBERS AND OTHER BUILDINGS WERE BUILT INTO THE OUTSIDE WALL. ABOUT 100 PEOPLE WOULD HAVE LIVED IN THE CASTLE.

snore

ZZZzz

Good Knight

Do you mind?

A "garderobe" was a toilet, and Bodiam Castle had about 30 of them!

A Medieval Banquet
All guests were given instructions on how to behave at the table.

I would like to make a toast

DO NOT:
SPIT ACROSS THE TABLE
FART
PICK YOUR NOSE
SCRATCH FLEA BITES

Slurp!

The banquet hall had two big fireplaces. Each one could roast a whole ox! *Almost every part of a pig was eaten* ... although not all at the one time! For entertainment, live birds would be put into a baked pie through a hole cut out of the bottom. The bird would then fly out when the pie was cut into! They liked to LARK about!

But they were allowed to throw bones on the floor.

That's Disgusting

stench

wiff

POOP CHUTE

Waste from the toilets ended up in the moat. With 30 of them, must have been very SMELLY!!!

16

BODIAM CASTLE 1388

BODIAM IS A QUADRANGULAR CASTLE, WITH CIRCULAR TOWERS ON EACH CORNER. IT WAS BUILT BY SIR EDWARD DALYNGRIGGE DURING THE HUNDRED YEARS WAR BETWEEN ENGLAND AND FRANCE. THE CASTLE STOOD GUARD OVER THE RIVER ROTHER TO DETER FRENCH RAIDERS, BUT WAS REALLY BUILT MORE AS A NICE HOME FOR THE POWERFUL KNIGHT AND HIS FAMILY. RICHARD III SENT SOLDIERS TO TAKE THE CASTLE IN 1483, BUT THE DEFENDERS SURRENDERED IT, WITH NO RECORDS OF A FIGHT TAKING PLACE.

snore

snore

Most of the buildings inside the castle were destroyed in 1644. It was during the English Civil War and Oliver Cromwell's men wanted to prevent the Royalists from using it as a base.

Good idea...two slices please!

Ye Olde Ketchup

Sir Munch Alot

Boo!

The ghostly figure of a **lady in red** has been seen gazing from a tower.

On the outside, the castle looks much the same as it did in 1388... but without the smelly moat!

The castle appears in the film – Monty Python and the Holy Grail, in which it was called "Swamp Castle". It has also been used in the filming of Dr Who.

I'm bored! I wish somebody would attack us!

pong

Keek-a Poo!

Terror-meter

17

During the "Hundred Years War" with France, the castle came under siege in 1377. The French tried everything to breach it, but up in the ramparts an expert Bowman, Peter de Heyno, had the French Commander in the sights of his silver crossbow.

Say Cheese!

Zilly English! Don't you mean fromage?

With **one deadly shot**, he killed the Commander and ended the siege. They still had to pay the French to leave though.

SIR FRANCIS DRAKE

C'mon England!

In 1588, the castle was heavily strengthened because of the threat from the Spanish Armada. Spain sent a fleet of 130 ships to invade England. Although they sailed very close to the island, Sir Francis Drake with 200 ships chased them off.

KABOOM!

SMASH

ENGLAND 1 - 0 SPAIN

Er! You any good at threading needles?

Here little fishy!

CHARLES I

Charles I got stuck between the window bars while trying to escape in 1647. He was imprisoned for 14 months, and was then beheaded in London. Oliver Cromwell allowed his head to be **sewn back** onto his body so the family could pay its respects. That was nice of Oliver!

OLIVER CROMWELL

CARISBROOKE CASTLE 1100

"Well, would you look at that!"

THE CASTLE iS OVER 800 YEARS OLD AND SiTUATED iN THE CENTRE OF THE iSLE OF WiGHT, OFF THE SOUTH COAST OF ENGLAND.

Henry I gave the original wooden castle to the De Redvers family in around 1100, and they began replacing it with stone.

In 1136, Baldwin de Redvers had to surrender the castle during a siege, because the castle well ran dry.

When he returned in 1253, he built a new well. The Countess Isabella de Redvers started making her own improvements from 1262, and was the first person in England to use glass in castle windows. The well in the castle is 49 meters (160ft) deep.

Prisoners were used to work a wooden tread wheel to bring up water. They were replaced by donkeys around 1690, which were used for hundreds of years. Donkeys can still be seen treading the wheel now ... well, not the exact same donkeys.

JACKASS!

The ghost of a **Grey Lady** wearing a long cloak has been seen. She floats along with four ghostly dogs on long leads.

The names of the donkeys all begin with "J", as this was how Charles I signed his letters while he was held prisoner at the castle

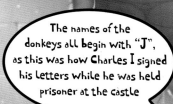

Terror-meter

A MUDDY SIEGE

After chasing the English invaders out of Scotland, the Scottish King **"Robert the Bruce"** tried to take the castle in 1315. For 11 days, the Scots struggled in heavy rain to set up a siege engine. The castle garrison was **very amused** to see all of this, and the Scots eventually gave up and trudged off back home.

ROBERT THE BRUCE

BUTCHER CUMBERLAND

In 1745, the Scottish Jacobites, led by **Bonnie Prince Charlie**, invaded England and attacked the castle. The defenders quickly surrendered and Prince Charlie's forces kept on going as far as Derby, where they were forced to retreat back to Scotland. A regiment was left behind to defend Carlisle Castle, but after 10 days, the Jacobites surrendered to the Duke of Cumberland.

The Duke — also known as "Butcher Cumberland" (any guesses why?) — had over 300 prisoners crammed into the dungeons. They were given no food or water, and many of them were **hung, drawn and quartered**. Today visitors can see the "licking-stones", where desperate prisoners licked the walls to obtain some moisture.

CARLISLE CASTLE 1122

CARLISLE CASTLE IS IN THE COUNTY OF CUMBRIA, NEAR THE BORDER WITH SCOTLAND.
SINCE THE ENGLISH AND SCOTS WERE ALWAYS FIGHTING THERE,
CARLISLE BECAME THE MOST BESIEGED CASTLE IN ENGLAND.

Yoo Hoo!

Mooo!

This is better than the circus

HAHAHA I love those guys

The stone castle was built mainly as a fortress in 1122, by Henry I.

When David I, the Scottish King, captured it in 1135, he completed the construction.

In 1568, **Mary Queen of Scots** was held prisoner within the castle for about two months.

In 1842, a soldier on guard was confronted by a **ghostly lady in white**. When he aimed his bayonet at her, she suddenly disappeared. The soldier fainted, and although he recovered, he **died of shock** shortly afterwards.

The secret is to keep your head!

It has been said that the Scottish song "The Bonnie Banks o' Loch Lomond" was written by a Jacobite soldier waiting to be hanged.

AHHHHH!

Is it my hair? I know, it's a frightful mess!

YOU COULD CALL THIS THE "TOWER OF YORK"

Like the Tower of London, it was often used as a prison and **place of execution**. In 1322, Roger de Clifford, who opposed Edward II, was hanged at the Tower for treason.

However, it was Henry VIII who used it the most. In 1537, the north of England was in **rebellion** against him. Hundreds of rebels and their leaders were executed at the castle.

One of the leaders, Robert Aske, was a London barrister, and came from an old Yorkshire family. Henry's men captured him and he was hanged in chains from a scaffold outside the Tower, and left to suffer a **slow death**. This was to be a warning to all other rebels.

I hate all this Hanging around!

Roger de Clifford

WHAT DO YOU MEAN there's no room at the Tower? Well... Stick him in the **CUPBOARD** then.

HENRY VIII

NO VACANCIES

Nooooo!!!! Not the Cupboard

It's use as a fortress came to an end in 1684, when to celebrate St George's Day, they had a gun salute on the roof of the tower. There was an **explosion** which set fire to the gunpowder room and destroyed the inside of the building.

The people of York hated the soldiers that controlled the castle. They gave Clifford's Tower the nickname "The Minced Pie", so many believed that the explosion had not been an accident. The town's folk celebrated the "Roasting of the Mince Pie", and the damage was never repaired.

William the Conqueror built **two castles in York.** The other one was 'Baile Hill' on the other side of the River Ouse.

Just a little something from the people of York!

Sniff! I'm... filling up!

Huh! I LOVE! pressies

CLIFFORD'S TOWER 1270

CLIFFORD'S TOWER IS ALMOST ALL THAT REMAINS OF YORK CASTLE. IN 1270, HENRY III PAID £2,600 TO HAVE IT BUILT, TOGETHER WITH A SURROUNDING WALL CONTAINING A GATEHOUSE AND TWO TOWERS.

In 1596, Robert Redhead was a jailer at the tower. To earn extra money he began demolishing the castle and selling the stones as building material.

To avoid getting caught, the **sneaky jailer** started on the inside. Luckily, he was stopped by the local council, or there would have been no Clifford's Tower and one very rich jailer!

Okay! Who's pinched the stairs?

OUCH!

Mummy!

Who's There?

Clever chap that jailer!

Yes...very clever! I wonder where he gets his stone?

JAILER LTD BUILDING MATERIALS

LIMITED STOCK

SALE

BOGOF

SOURCED LOCALLY

Grrrrrrr

York is said to be the most haunted city in Britain, but it seems like the ghosts were too busy to visit The Tower'

That's not my fault... I've got "no body" to go with!

Terror-meter

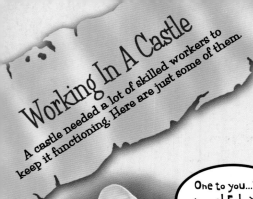

Working In A Castle

A castle needed a lot of skilled workers to keep it functioning. Here are just some of them.

Cooper
Barrel maker

BIGGER! hammer!

Might need a bigger hammer!

Blacksmith
Producer of ironworks and horse shoes

Biller
Axe maker

One to you...Two to me! Er!...YES! Can I help you?

Carpenter
Builds roofing, furniture and siege engines

Clerk
Keeps accounts of wages and cost of materials

Scullion
Kitchen cleaner and dishwasher

I'm sure these will help get my POINT across!

Cottar
A peasant who did odd jobs

Cobbler
Makes and repairs shoes

Fletcher
Arrow maker

Now don't worry madam! The drink is in capiboo..capabu.. very good hands! HIC!

Constable
Took charge of the castle while the owner was away

Bottler
In charge of drinks storage

Chandler
Candle maker

YE OLDE WORDSEARCH

Will someone save me from the Puzzle Palace!

I'll save you Princess... Where's my legs gone?

URGENT

Knight In Shining Armour required!

Please contact the Princess.

Text: 1066

How do you make the poor happy?

Give them a peasant surprise!

long live The King...

arrghhhhh!

...oops! too late.

This Yours?

```
N Y J O V M R F B A V C R S F N Y Z
C W V T M Q Y L Z G S T N B V R C H
L O D K C L E R K N C D B Y D X O L
V Z B Q A R F D P T U H L O F U T G
P L N B C O O P E R L Q A W C J T U
H R O P L V Z Y L B L F C V A D A Z
N B C J W E N F C Z I P K G R Z R O
Y D Z A B M R U W T O X S Y P N H T
D C O N S T A B L E N F M B E L X Q
A R B X G V U H Y S L R I S N C B O
Z O Y I N M F A V B Y N T Z T R P Y
M L K U L C R L P E O F H P E U F T
F H Q V R L T G E Z J T W L R H O V
R N C A J P E S M T Y P T D N G L D
T S D P Q B Y R D H C Q M L Y T X N
U C H A N D L E R B O H U K E B H O
P T S V Z Q M S E N F L E G M R Y L
L U C X I Y J F C L T D N R V C E B
```

The Names Can be Found Down, Across & Diagonally

Why did King Arthur make his table round?

To cut corners.

Wonder if they need some **CHOPPING!** done?

Brave Lady Bankes

During the violent English Civil War, Sir John Bankes had left his wife to protect the castle while he visited the King.

But Sir John, aren't you afraid the Roundheads might attack the castle?

Ohhh!...I see! Poor devils!

Nope... I've left my wife in charge!

How many men do they have captain?

Only eighty Sir! But...they have seven women!

Curses, we might as well go home then!

It came under siege in 1643 when **Lady Bankes and her daughters only had 80 men** to defend them against 600 Roundheads. The Roundheads attacked with siege ladders, but as they rushed up, the defenders threw hot embers over their heads, which soon stopped them.

Two years later, and with Sir John Bankes dead, Corfe Castle was one of the last Royalist strongholds in the south of England. This time, 500 Roundheads arrived to lay siege to the castle and **Lady Bankes had to defend it again.** She fought them off bravely for 7 weeks, until one of her own soldiers pretended to go for more men, sneakily returning with Roundheads in disguise. They attacked the Royalists from the inside, taking them all by surprise.

WAIT! I can get you in the castle, just don't tell Lady Bankes!!!

Brave Lady Bankes and the garrison were allowed to leave, but the Government had the castle blown apart. The villagers were pleased to build new houses with the hundreds of scattered stones.

BOOM

I've got it! I've got it!

CORFE CASTLE 1087

CORFE CASTLE SITS ATOP A 55 METRE (180FT) HIGH HILL, AND COULD BE SEEN FROM MILES AWAY. ITS DEFENDERS COULD ALSO SEE FOR MILES, WHICH WAS QUITE HANDY. CORFE WAS PROBABLY ONE OF THE FIRST CASTLES TO BE BUILT IN STONE DURING THE REIGN OF WILLIAM THE CONQUEROR, BETWEEN 1066 AND 1087.

Are you feeling alright Lady Bankes?

Yes...I just had a bad corfe!

BY 1105, HIS SON, HENRY I, HAD ERECTED THE CASTLE KEEP AND OTHER DEFENCES, AND KING JOHN THEN TRANSFORMED IT INTO A ROYAL PALACE.

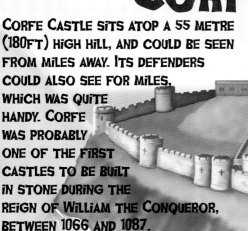

When it was just a wooden castle, back in 975, a young King Edward was out hunting nearby when he became separated from his attendants.

His **evil aunt** Elfrida offered him a drink, and then had him killed while still on his horse. As the king tried to get away, he got his foot stuck in the stirrup and was dragged along until he died.

Twenty-five French knights were held here in 1202, but after an escape attempt, twenty-two of them were recaptured, thrown into the dungeon and **starved to death**.

food, I need food! Quick...pass me a can opener.

The ghost of a headless woman has been seen wandering around the castle gates.

LOOK WHERE I'M GOING WILL YOU?

Terror-meter

Between 1179 and 1188, King Henry II spent a vast amount of money rebuilding the castle. He built the massive stone Keep, with walls up to 6.5 meter (21ft) thick. The Keep is surrounded by an outer wall and an inner wall, with towers. It was an **awesome sight** to any approaching ships.

Henry also had it designed as a **grand palace**, to impress visiting royalty, and other very important religious people when they landed in England.

KEEP OUT

Very impressive!

What a grand palace!

We'll jump out when they arrive!

Ohhh! I LOVE! Surprises

What's french for "GO AWAY!"

BE QUIET

Really??? That can't be right!

shhh!

Oh dear!

KING HENRY II

I built that!

The walls of the Great Tower are about 25.3 meters (83ft) high.

The **White Cliffs** of Dover are over 100 meters (350ft) high and are made of white chalk.

Johnny English was filmed here in 2003

First Baron's War

In 1216, Prince Louis of **France invaded England**, and gained control of London and all the South-East, except for Dover Castle and Windsor Castle.

The French soldiers laid siege to Dover Castle on 19th July. Although they did manage to break down an outer wall, the English tunnelled out through the soft rock to fight them. Eventually, after months of fighting, **the French gave up the siege** on 14th October and a truce was agreed.

LOUIS VIII

Curse you English and your fancy pants castle!

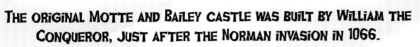

DOVER CASTLE 1179 – 1188

BUILT MAINLY AS A FORTRESS TO GUARD THE SHORTEST SEA CROSSING BETWEEN ENGLAND AND THE EUROPEAN MAINLAND, DOVER CASTLE SITS ON THE TOWERING "WHITE CLIFFS" ON THE KENT COASTLINE.

THE ORIGINAL MOTTE AND BAILEY CASTLE WAS BUILT BY WILLIAM THE CONQUEROR, JUST AFTER THE NORMAN INVASION IN 1066.

During the Napoleonic Wars at the end of the 18th century, there was a constant threat of invasion.

Tunnels were made under the castle to house 2,000 soldiers, ready to fight at any time, but the invasion never came. There are believed to be over three miles of tunnels.

NAPOLEON BONAPARTE

Vive la France!

People wonder why Napoleon kept one hand inside his jacket...

Maybe he was keeping his chips warm!

Can you see the back end?

YES!

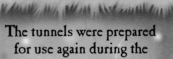

The tunnels were prepared for use again during the **Second World War**, both as an underground hospital, and also as the command centre for the evacuation of troops from Dunkirk, in France, in May, 1940.

You've hit a pipe...

stupid boy!

DANGER! DO NOT GET WET

In 1802, Sean O'Flynn, a 14-year-old drummer boy was carrying money on an errand. He was attacked and beheaded by men from his own regiment. When his body was discovered, the head could not be found. Since then, the sound of drumming has been heard, and there have also been sightings of his headless figure walking around.

After a couple of sieges during the English Civil War, the owner of the castle was persuaded to hand it over to Royalists by his cousin who was a Royalist cavalier. However, by 1645, the Royalists were losing and the castle came under siege from Cromwell's forces this time.

The attackers planted three mines under the castle walls, but still failed to damage them. The garrison eventually gave up and surrendered the castle after five months.

CLUNK

Ohh! Chocolate raisins!

Right! Let's get out of here before it blows!

Dunster Castle Slighting

"Slighting" a castle is to partly destroy it, so that it can't be used again for defensive purposes. During and after the English Civil War, nearly 60 castles were slighted by the Government — many of them on the orders of Oliver Cromwell — to prevent the Royalists from using them again. This is the reason why there are so many ruined castles throughout England.

You idiots! You've demolished the wrong castle!

OLIVER CROMWELL

When Dunster Castle's walls were slighted, in 1650, it took 200 men 12 days to turn them into piles of rubble, but the Mansion and the Gatehouse were saved.

DUNSTER CASTLE 12TH CENTURY

ORIGINALLY THE SITE OF A SAXON FORT, THE CASTLE SITS ON TOP OF A HILL, NEAR THE SEA IN SOMERSET. THE ORIGINAL STONE SHELL KEEP WAS ERECTED BY WILLIAM DE MOHUN, IN THE EARLY 12TH CENTURY, AND WITHSTOOD A HARD SIEGE DURING THE CIVIL WAR KNOWN AS "THE ANARCHY".

Anarchy means no government in charge

IT HAS BEEN OWNED BY JUST TWO FAMILIES OVER A PERIOD OF 900 YEARS. AFTER HER HUSBAND'S DEATH IN 1375, LADY JOAN DE MOHUN FELT IT WAS TOO DRAUGHTY AND SOLD THE CASTLE TO LADY ELIZABETH LUTTRELL. THE LUTTRELL FAMILY OWNED IT FOR THE FOLLOWING 600 YEARS, BUILDING THE IMPOSING GATEHOUSE IN AROUND 1400.

The ghost of a Royalist soldier has been seen wandering the rooms and corridors of the castle.

Creepy Dunster

I'm not wandering! I'm looking for the loo if you must know!

HUH...Grey! Why's it always grey! Why can't it be cerise pink or lemony yellow?

There have been sightings of a **Grey Lady** in various rooms, but she has appeared mainly on the Grand Staircase. Visitors have told of being tapped on the shoulder, but when they turned round there was no one there. (Sounds like the school prankster!)

The skeleton of a man about 7 feet tall was found in an enclosed pit dungeon.

He had been chained to the wall and left there to die.

So... they stretched you first then?

Nope!

You should see my big brother!

7ft

6ft

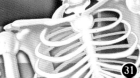

Life in the Castle

In the year 1385–86, over £1,000 was spent on food and drink.

In that year the castle brought in 28,567 gallons of ale, 4,377 gallons of wine, 70,321 loaves of bread, 150 sheep, 40 barrels of herring, 1,866 fish, 656 rabbits, 1,159 chickens and 90 deer.

On a single day, in 1428, about 85 people living in the castle consumed: 176 loaves of bread; 84 gallons of ale; 133¼ gallons of wine; 20 oxen; 4 sheep; and 25 chickens.

So that's 2 loaves of bread, ¼ of a chicken and ¼ of an ox, plus 1 gallon of ale and 1½ gallons of wine each! Or even more for some, if others didn't eat their entire share! Gluttons!

Okay! That's the lot...where do you want it?

Eh!.... My room!

Framlingham

Roland the Farter

At Hemingstone Manor, not far from Framlingham, lived a famous flatulist **(professional farter)** and entertainer of the 12th century: Roland the Farter.

Parrrrrp! Frooooottt! Tooot! Squeaak!

BRAVO!

KING HENRY II

SNIFF!

Can you smell gas?

Haahaahaa! Brilliant!

King Henry II allowed Roland to live in the Manor and have 30 acres of land in return for performing as a jester at Christmas. So each year, Roland would perform **"one jump, one whistle and one fart"** at the King's Christmas party.

FRAMLINGHAM CASTLE 1214

FRAMLINGHAM CASTLE, IN SUFFOLK, IS AN IMPRESSIVE LOOKING FORTRESS, WITH 13 TOWERS DOMINATING ITS HUGE OUTSIDE WALL. THE STONE CASTLE WAS BUILT BY ROGER BIGOD, THE EARL OF NORFOLK, IN AROUND 1213, REPLACING THE ORIGINAL MOTTE AND BAILEY TIMBER CASTLE. UNLIKE MOST OTHER CASTLES OF THE TIME THERE WAS NO CENTRAL KEEP.

No Mary!... I am not going to paper the walls!

IN 1215, ROGER BIGOD REBELLED AGAINST KING JOHN IN THE FIRST BARONS' WAR. THE CASTLE SOON CAME UNDER SIEGE, AND IT WAS A SURPRISE WHEN THE GARRISON OF 53 MEN SURRENDERED THIS MASSIVE NEW FORTRESS WITHOUT A FIGHT. I GUESS THEY SAW THAT KING JOHN WAS IN ONE OF HIS NASTY MOODS.

When Edward VI died, in 1553, his sister Mary should have been the rightful Queen of England. However, John Dudley, the Duke of Northumberland, proclaimed his daughter-in-law, Lady Jane Grey, as the new Queen of England instead. Mary claimed that the throne belonged to her, and sensing that her life could be in danger, she moved to Framlingham Castle with her military guard. Support for Mary grew throughout the country, and after only nine days as queen, Lady Jane was deposed and, at last, Mary became Queen of England.

Both John Dudley and Lady Jane were eventually beheaded at the Tower of London.

That's the last time I listen to you!

When's the show starting? Cool... 3D!

LIVE Beheading Today at 3pm SHARP!

QUEEN MARY

Heehee! It's the last time she's going to listen to anyone!...EVER!

Terror-meter

KENILWORTH CASTLE 1125

MANY DIFFERENT KINGS KEPT ADDING BITS TO KENILWORTH CASTLE, MAKING IT A HUGE FORTRESS. THE OLDEST PART OF THE CASTLE IS THE 24 METER (80FT) KEEP, BUILT BY GEOFFREY DE CLINTON. WHEN KING JOHN TOOK OWNERSHIP OF IT IN THE EARLY 12TH CENTURY, HE SPENT A HUGE SUM OF MONEY REBUILDING THE OUTSIDE WALLS AND TOWERS. HE ALSO CREATED A MERE (A LARGE SHALLOW LAKE) AROUND IT, TO STRENGTHEN ITS DEFENCES.

What do you get if you cross a Sheepdog with a Tulip?... A Collie-flower!

A Long Siege

During the Second Barons' War in 1265, Baron Loyalists used the castle as their base. When their leader, Simon de Montfort, agreed to surrender to King Henry III, the king's envoy was sent to get the keys. Instead, Simon had the **man's hand cut off** and sent him back to the king.

RIGHT! Who did it?

Pssst!

This made King Henry furious and he set out to besiege the castle. It became the **longest siege in English history**, and for 6 months, its garrison endured a heavy assault. The king's men built huge wooden towers for archers, crept up on barges at night, and pounded it with huge stones. In the end, the garrison surrendered because of illness and starvation.

Robert Dudley, the Earl of Leicester, was a very close friend of Queen Elizabeth I, and wanted to marry her. So, to impress her, he **spent loads of money** making the castle nice, including luxurious living quarters for the queen and her escorts to stay in, when they visited.

He decided to **spend a lot more money** on a huge 19-day festival for the queen. He put on a magnificent firework display and a play staged on the lake with a 5 meter (18ft) floating mermaid. After the event, Robert didn't have much money left, and he never did get to marry the queen, but what a fantastic party they had!

Grrrrrrr!

Awww... look at the little bear... who's a cute little fellow then?

ROBERT DUDLEY

QUEEN ELIZABETH

THE GHOSTLY GATEHOUSE

The phantom figure of an old lady has been seen in the gatehouse, breaking the same candle over and over again. It is said that a man in black, who was killed in a sword fight, also roams the gatehouse. Maybe he is looking for a match for the old lady's candle.

What do you mean it doesn't look that bad?

Terror-meter

LANCASTER CASTLE 1170

LANCASTER CASTLE IS SITUATED IN THE CENTRE OF LANCASTER, ON THE SITE OF AN OLD ROMAN FORT. THE KEEP WAS BUILT AROUND 1170, FOLLOWED BY THE WELL TOWER IN 1325. INSIDE THE TOWER ARE TWO WELLS AND THREE UNDERGROUND DUNGEONS. THE FORMIDABLE TWIN-TOWERED GATEHOUSE WAS ADDED BY KING HENRY IV, IN 1399.

Na-ha ha-ha-ha!

OOH! Just you wait...!

Tell me honestly, will I be okay?

Nah!

Eh?

The Pendle Witches

In 1612, ten people were convicted at the castle, and **executed for murder and witchcraft.** Giving evidence was nine-year-old Jennet Device, who accused her mother, brother and four others of using witchcraft. They were all found guilty and were hanged at "Gallows Hill", on the moors above the town.

GASP!

HORROR!

YOO HOO!

My dear child, please tell the courtroom... When did you realise they were Witches?

When they told me to tidy my room!

Readit!

In the 19th century you could be hanged for burglary, horse-stealing, highway robbery, forging banknotes, or even for taking one little sheep. Oops! I almost forgot ... and for being a WITCH, like me!

Hee...Hee...Hee!

Pay the Jailer

For hundreds of years the castle was used as a Prison and a Courthouse. In the 16th century, the Jailer didn't get a wage and got his income from the prisoners, who would **pay him for better treatment**, such as having chains removed, or maybe having an extra portion of food. The more you were able to pay, the more treats you got...even having your friends visit you for a party.

NEXT!

Branding Baddies

Around 1800, a Branding Iron was used on convicted prisoners. The red-hot Iron branded the letter "M" onto the convict's hand. So when a person went on trial they had to raise their hand in front of the judge. If it had an "M" on it, the judge knew they had been convicted before. The "M" meant that the accused person was a "Malefactor"; an evil-doer.

Honest your honour, er!... It's a...w!

Guards, please tell the prisoner to turn his hand... the other way!

TSSSSSS

Old Ned Barlow

From 1800, hanging took place beside the castle, in an area known as "Hanging Corner". Crowds of up to 5,000 people would gather to watch the gruesome events. A well-known Hangman at the time was Old Ned Barlow, who handled over **130 executions**. He died in the prison in 1812, after being imprisoned for stealing a horse. Lucky he wasn't hanged! Many criminals were transported to Australia as a punishment, which was better than being hanged.

Yes very lucky ... I guess!

Terror-meter

LEEDS CASTLE 1119

LEEDS CASTLE IS SITUATED IN THE COUNTY OF KENT (NOT YORKSHIRE), JUST 40 MILES FROM LONDON.

In 1321, King Edward II besieged the castle because the Baron's wife that had been left in charge of it, would not allow the King's wife Isabella and her escorts to stop there. Six of Isabella's men were killed by archers from the castle.

When the castle was taken, the Baron's wife was imprisoned in the Tower of London. Even though he had not even been there, her husband was executed anyway. It is believed that it was all a ploy so that Isabella could have the castle.

Edward now had an excuse to attack and take the castle.

Eh!...The Baroness says, the place is a bit of a mess... Can you come back later?

That's it! I'm telling the King on you!

FOOL!

Welcome To The DUNGEON
PLEASE DIE QUIETLY

Now Remember! DON'T! start the fire until every man is freed!

OOPS!

During a civil war in 1666, 600 Dutch and French prisoners of war were held there. In an effort to escape they set the castle on fire, causing severe damage.

NOSEY!

In the Middle Ages there was no piped water in castles. A large barrel cut in half was used for a bath.

POP

Margaret: wife of King Edward I
Isabella: wife of Edward II
Anne of Bohemia: 1st wife of Richard II
Joan of Navarre: 2nd wife of Henry IV
Catherine de Valois: wife of Henry V
Catherine of Aragon: 1st wife of King Henry VIII

CATHERINE DE VALOIS

JOAN OF NAVARRE

Leeds is now a glorious castle again, fit for a queen.

Thanks to Lady Ballie, an American heiress, who bought it in 1927.

The original stone castle was built by Robert de Crevecoeur in 1119 as a stronghold for the Normans.

It is believed to be King Edward I who created the lake to make it a more grand place to stay.

King Henry VIII transformed it into a palace for his first wife, Catherine of Aragon.

I did it all for you my dear... Well..., you only get married once!

Ten quid for a castle! What a bargain!

After all the queens had lived in it, the castle was given to Sir Anthony St Leger in 1552 for a yearly rent of £10. Leeds is now a glorious castle again, **fit for a queen**. Thanks to Lady Ballie, an American heiress, who bought it in 1927.

Lots of very important people still hold important meetings there.

£10

Oh Henry... It's wonderful. I shall take great care of it.

Well if you don't... it might be a CHOP for dinner.

Terror-meter

For over 900 years, Lincoln Castle was used as a prison. In the 18th century, most of the prisoners were just people who had failed to pay their debts. If they had money they could pay the Jailer to give them an easy time, but if they had no money the Jailer could be very nasty. Even the very young were detained at the castle, such as 11-year-old Walter Meadows, who was imprisoned in 1877, for stealing 5 shillings. This could have bought him 100 eggs, or a licence for a dog.

Crime and Transportation

In the 19th century, criminals were still being executed, but many were sentenced to be transported to other counties. Quite often, their crimes were not very serious.

John Brocksom: a butcher; convicted of stealing 7 sheep; transported to Australia in 1840.

Joseph Ashton: convicted of stealing a lamb; sentenced to life; transported to Australia in 1835.

William Bray: convicted of stealing a shovel (had 3 previous convictions); sentenced to 7 years; transported to Australia in 1829.

Francis Buttery: a labourer; convicted of stealing a dead pig (with no head or insides); transported to Bermuda in 1823.

William Chapman: aged 16; convicted of Highway Robbery; sentenced to death, but transported to Australia in 1816.

LINCOLN CASTLE
12TH CENTURY

THE CASTLE SITS ON THE SITE OF THE ROMAN FORT OF LINDUM. LINCOLN WAS ONE OF ENGLAND'S MAJOR TOWNS WHEN THE NORMANS DECIDED TO BUILD A TIMBER CASTLE THERE IN 1068. THEY TORE DOWN 166 HOUSES TO MAKE ROOM FOR IT, WHICH MADE THEM VERY UNPOPULAR.

THE TIMBER FORT WAS BADLY DAMAGED AFTER THE FIRST BATTLE OF LINCOLN, AND WAS REPLACED BY THE LUCY TOWER IN 1141. IT IS ONE OF ONLY TWO CASTLES TO HAVE TWO MOTTES.

Oi!...who goes there?

Clunk!

NORMANS GO HOME!

Psst...over ere! We're being watched

But my name's Norman!

Snigger

Ha ha ha

Ohh yesss! Kind of ugly aint they!

The Magna Carta

Lincoln Castle holds one of only four copies of this 13th-century document. Magna Carta (Great Charter) was an agreement drawn up in 1215, following the First Barons' War between King John and the powerful English Barons. It gave rights to the people of England.

King John would put innocent people in prison and steal their belongings and land. The Barons wanted to stop this and have people judged fairly by their peers.

King John didn't want to sign the document, but he needed the support of the Barons to remain in power. It was said that the King was so annoyed that, after signing it, he went home, closed the door, and then rolled around the floor screaming, in a mad fit of rage.

No! No! No!

He seems to be taking it quite well.

Terror-meter

Siege Engines

Big! Innit

The Trebuchet

Invented by the Chinese around 300 BC, the Trebuchet could do serious damage to a castle by hurling large stones at its walls and towers. It was also used to throw balls of burning material into the castle to cause fires, or maybe **dead animals such as pigs and cows** would be used to cause illness and spread diseases. Sometimes the attackers would constantly hurl the objects into the castle day and night to cause as much distress as possible.

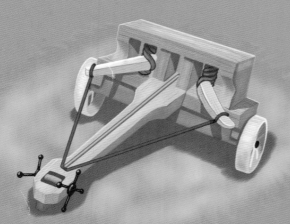

The Ballista

The Ballista was like a **giant crossbow** and was designed to fire a bolt or javelin at opposing soldiers. Being easy to move around, it could be placed on top of a castle tower.

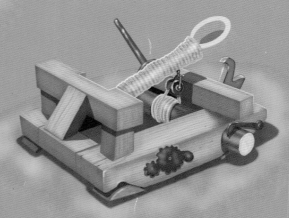

The Mangonel

Although it wasn't very accurate, the Mangonel was powerful and fast. It could **hurl heavy objects** at castle walls, or be used by the castle defenders to destroy the attackers siege weapons.

SIEGE THE DIFFERENCE

CAN YOU SPOT THE 12 DIFFERENCES BETWEEN THESE TWO DRAWINGS?

Prisoners of Pontefract

In the Middle Ages, Pontefract Castle was known as "Pomfret Castle". It was a vast fortress and one of the strongest castles in England. Above ground it became a grand palace, but underneath it was a **terrifying prison.**

Prisoners would be taken 11 meters (35ft) down into its large underground network of Dungeons. One of them was down a steep passageway, and across a plank of wood placed over a Bottomless Pit. On the other side, was a cell where the prisoners were **shut away in total darkness.**

"Sometimes I would make them walk the plank ... just for fun!"

In 1322, King Edward II had his cousin Thomas, the Earl of Lancaster, publicly executed for treason.

The Earl was the owner of Pontefract Castle, and it may have been the last thing he saw as he was beheaded outside it. Twenty other rebels were given the same treatment.

King Richard II was held in the castle in 1399, until his death was announced a year later. No one knows what happened to him, although it is thought that he was murdered, or maybe starved to death.

BOO!

Happy Hour this Friday! Bring Your Own PLAGUE!

But I can't swim!

5.9

6.0

ARGHH

That's okay, there's no water in it! Hee Hee Hee!

But we're cousins...

Well I did say I would make you "Head of the family"

Murder here, beheading there... Can't we have a nice ending for a change?

PONTEFRACT CASTLE 1204

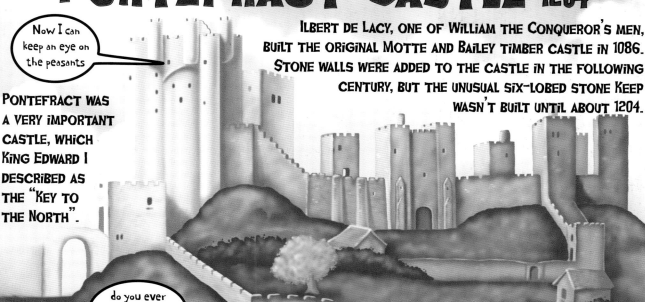

Now I can keep an eye on the peasants

ILBERT DE LACY, ONE OF WILLIAM THE CONQUEROR'S MEN, BUILT THE ORIGINAL MOTTE AND BAILEY TIMBER CASTLE IN 1086. STONE WALLS WERE ADDED TO THE CASTLE IN THE FOLLOWING CENTURY, BUT THE UNUSUAL SIX-LOBED STONE KEEP WASN'T BUILT UNTIL ABOUT 1204.

PONTEFRACT WAS A VERY IMPORTANT CASTLE, WHICH KING EDWARD I DESCRIBED AS THE "KEY TO THE NORTH".

do you ever feel you're being watched?

It came under siege a few times during the English Civil War, but it was never taken by force.

The people of Pontefract hated the castle, as they always suffered during the sieges. So when the Civil War ended in 1649, they asked the Government to destroy it. Oliver Cromwell, who had defeated the Royalists, also wanted to get rid of it, as it had been so **difficult to besiege**. So the castle was taken apart, leaving just some scattered ruins.

If it had been left intact, it would have been one of the **most impressive castles in Britain**.

But the dungeons still exist

Help

Stink

The ghost of a tall man carrying an axe has been seen walking around the ruins.

HA! HA! HA!

Terror-meter

Prisoners of War

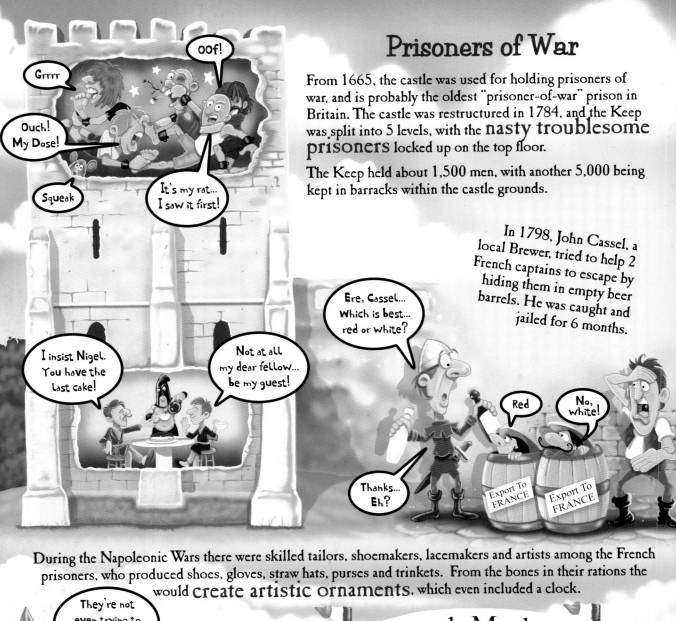

From 1665, the castle was used for holding prisoners of war, and is probably the oldest "prisoner-of-war" prison in Britain. The castle was restructured in 1784, and the Keep was split into 5 levels, with the **nasty troublesome prisoners** locked up on the top floor.

The Keep held about 1,500 men, with another 5,000 being kept in barracks within the castle grounds.

In 1798, John Cassel, a local Brewer, tried to help 2 French captains to escape by hiding them in empty beer barrels. He was caught and jailed for 6 months.

During the Napoleonic Wars there were skilled tailors, shoemakers, lacemakers and artists among the French prisoners, who produced shoes, gloves, straw hats, purses and trinkets. From the bones in their rations the would **create artistic ornaments**, which even included a clock.

French Market

There were regular open days in the castle yard for prisoners to sell or exchange their wares with local people, who would bring dairy products, home-made bread and other items.

PORTCHESTER CASTLE 11TH CENTURY

THE CASTLE IS SITUATED IN A NATURAL HARBOUR, AT PORTSMOUTH ON THE SOUTH COAST. ITS WALLS WERE BUILT BY THE ROMANS IN THE 3RD CENTURY, AND IT IS REPUTED TO BE THE BEST EXAMPLE OF A ROMAN FORT IN BRITAIN.

How do you cut the Roman Empire down to size? With a pair of Caesars!

FORMING A SQUARE, THE WALLS ARE ABOUT 20FT HIGH AND 5FT THICK, AND ORIGINALLY HAD 20 BASTIONS SPREAD EVENLY AROUND THEM, BUT ONLY 14 HAVE SURVIVED.

Oi! NORMAN! Watch it!

After the Normans conquered England, William Mauduit built the first stone castle in around 1136, with the Great Tower being built in stages, and reaching a height of over 100ft by the 14th century.

Wait for me!

France

For hundreds of years, Portchester was used regularly by royalty, and also by English armies travelling to and from France. Edward III and his 15,000-strong army assembled there to depart for France in 1346, and went on to defeat the French at the famous "Battle of Crecy".

By 1400, Richard II had spent almost £2,000 turning it into a grand palace, which was a lot of money. It became popular with royalty, and was used by Elizabeth I to hold court in 1601.

Hurry up you lot or we'll miss the boat!

Terror-meter

In 1215, about 100 rebel soldiers tried to hold the castle against King John. Using five huge siege engines, the king's men battered the castle with big stones. But when that didn't work, they undermined a corner of the castle, and **used the fat from 40 pigs** to set the wooden mine props on fire.

When the corner came crashing down, a fierce battle was fought as the King's men tried to enter the castle, but the defenders fought them off. As the siege continued, the rebels were desperate for food and **resorted to eating their horses.** Eventually, after a seven-week siege, the starving rebels surrendered.

King John was furious that the rebels were able to hold out for so long, and ordered that a **monument be built to honour the 40 pigs.**

During "The Peasants' Revolt", in 1381, the castle came under attack from thousands of peasants. The castle surrendered, and was then looted by the angry mob.

ROCHESTER CASTLE 1127

LIKE MANY CASTLES, ROCHESTER WAS BUILT ON THE SITE OF AN OLD ROMAN FORT. IT GUARDED A MAJOR ROAD ACROSS THE RIVER MEDWAY, BETWEEN DOVER AND LONDON.

THE NORMANS BUILT A MOTTE AND BAILEY TIMBER CASTLE HERE, SOON AFTER THEIR VICTORY AT THE BATTLE OF HASTINGS IN 1066.

All clear captain!

IT WAS ONE OF THE FIRST TIMBER CASTLES TO BE REPLACED BY STONE, WHEN WILLIAM II REBUILT ITS DEFENCES IN 1089. SOME YEARS LATER, AROUND 1127, THE HUGE TOWER WAS ERECTED. IT IS 34 METERS (113FT) HIGH AND THE TALLEST CASTLE KEEP IN ENGLAND.

In 1264, Lady Blanche de Warrene was **killed accidentally** by her husband-to-be, Ralph de Capo.

An unwanted suitor, Sir Gilbert Clare, confronted Lady Blanche on the battlements of the castle. Watching from a distance, Ralph thought she was in danger and fired an arrow at him.

OOPS!

He hit his target, but the arrow bounced off Ralph's armour and struck Lady Blanche. It went straight through her heart and killed her.

The ghostly figure of Lady Blanche has been seen walking across the battlements with the arrow still in her.

Well isn't that just great! This dress was brand new!

Terror-meter

John Clifford, the 9th Lord of Skipton, was known as "The Butcher". His father had been killed by the Duke of York's forces, at the Battle of St Albans, in 1455, and he **wanted revenge.** Five years later, Clifford managed to capture the Duke's son and killed him, then hacked off his head and impaled it on a spike on the walls of York. Clifford even placed a paper crown on top of the head to mock the Duke's young son's claim to the throne. This was the evil deed that earned him his nickname.

The Butcher

Ahhh! Now I see why they call you the BUTCHER.... It's the apron isn't it?

Water... we need water!

But Captain, the well is full of water!

We'll wait them out. Without water they'll give up in a matter of days! Hahahaha!

Shushhh... you fool!

Yeah! Stupid Royalists... Hahahaha!

Skipton Castle was the **last royal stronghold** in the north to withstand the Parliamentary troops during the Civil War (probably owing to a well within the castle, which has only recently been discovered). The castle eventually surrendered to Oliver Cromwell after three long years. He ordered the removal of the roofs and the slighting of the walls, so that the Royalists could not use it again as a Fortress.

However, 10 years later, Lady Anne Clifford was allowed to rebuild it on condition that the walls were not too thick, and the roof was not strong enough to take the weight of a cannon.

Everything seems in Order Lady Clifford, just remember... No Cannons!

Cannons!.. Never! Err...heehee... No cannons here!

SKIPTON CASTLE 12TH CENTURY

IN 1090, ROBERT DE ROMILLE, A NORMAN BARON, BUILT THE FIRST TIMBER CASTLE TO DEFEND AGAINST SCOTTISH RAIDS INTO ENGLAND. IT WASN'T MUCH GOOD, SO IT WAS SOON REPLACED BY A FORMIDABLE STONE CASTLE, WITH A SERIES OF CIRCULAR DRUM TOWERS. THE STEEP CLIFFS BEHIND THE CASTLE HELPED TO STRENGTHEN ITS DEFENCES.

King Edward II gave the castle to the Clifford family in 1310, and it was held by the family for over 350 years. They strengthened the castle, enabling it to withstand a long siege during the Civil War.

Stonemasons' marks can be found in the stonework at the main entrance and in the Conduit Court. These very skilled workers would travel across Europe, building and carving in stone. At one time, they were paid by the number of stones that they carved. Each stonemason had their own special mark or initial to put on a stone, to ensure they got paid.

Terror-meter

51

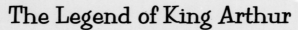

The Legend of King Arthur

Tintagel has been called the Birthplace of King Arthur who, as the legend says, ruled England in the 5th century. Arthur was married to Guinevere and established the famous "Knights of the Round Table". He was said to be protected from evil by **Merlin the Wizard**, who lived in a cave at the foot of the cliff.

The Sword in the Stone

The legend says that to be the true heir to the throne of England, a person had to pull the sword **Excalibur** from an anvil set in stone. Inscribed on the sword were the words: "Who so pulleth out this sword from this stone and anvil is right wise king born of all England". Or in simple terms: "Whoever pulls this sword out, will get crowned!"

Many small, strong men tried to pull the sword out, and many BIG strong men tried too, but it didn't move an inch. Then Arthur, who was only a boy, stood over the stone and removed the sword. **Easy-peasy!** The crowd cheered and Arthur was the rightful King of England.

TINTAGEL CASTLE 1233

TINTAGEL CASTLE LOOKS AS IF IT IS ON AN ISLAND, AS IT SITS HIGH ON THE TOP OF RUGGED CLIFFS, BUT IT IS ACTUALLY ON THE MAINLAND OF CORNWALL. IT WAS BUILT BY RICHARD, THE EARL OF CORNWALL, IN 1233.,

UNLIKE MOST OTHER CASTLES, IT HAS NO STRATEGIC IMPORTANCE FOR DEFENSIVE PURPOSES, AND WAS ERECTED MAINLY TO HONOUR THE LEGEND OF TINTAGEL, AS THE BIRTHPLACE OF KING ARTHUR.

Who invented King Arthur's round table?

Sir Cumference!

Hmmm... Could be a clue!

King Arthur

King Arthur

Arthur HERE!

Arthur was here

In 1998, excavations near the castle found a stone that seems to have "Arthur" written on it. So, the mystery about this being King Arthur's castle is more believable.

A Roman-style leather purse containing ten Roman coins has also been unearthed near the castle.

It is said that the ghost of Merlin haunts the cave at the bottom of the cliffs.

WOOOOOOOH! Wait a minute! GHOST! what do you mean ghost?

Terror-meter

TOWER OF LONDON 1078 – 1100

THE HUGE WHITE TOWER WAS BUILT BY WILLIAM THE CONQUEROR AFTER HE WAS CROWNED KING OF ENGLAND. IT TOOK YEARS TO BUILD AND WAS COMPLETED BY 1100. KING WILLIAM WANTED TO SHOW HOW POWERFUL HE WAS, AND THE TOWER LOOKED AWESOME TO THE PEOPLE OF LONDON.

TODAY, THE TOWER IS USED TO KEEP AND DISPLAY THE CROWN JEWELS.

BEEFEATERS

The guards at the tower are called "Yeomen Warders", but they have been nicknamed "Beefeaters"

We were once given beef as part of our wages, so that could be where our nickname comes from.

I thought they would have eaten 'Blackbirds Baked in a Pie'

God save the king

WILLIAM THE CONQUEROR

The guards red uniform includes emblems of a thistle, a rose and a shamrock for Scotland, England and Ireland.

Oh, that's me!

There are six Ravens which can always be found in the grounds of the tower. Around 1675, King Charles II was warned that the Kingdom of England would fall if they were removed. He ordered that six be kept at all times. Each bird has its wings clipped, so that it can't fly away.

Every day they are fed on beef and biscuits... soaked in BLOOD! YUK!

Can you find six Ravens on these pages? Don't include me.

Six ravens died from stress during the Second World War bombing of London

54

For over 900 years, the castle has been used for many purposes: it has been a fortress in times of war; a Royal Mint for producing money; a royal residence; a menagerie for keeping wild animals and an observatory. However, it is best known as a prison and a place for executions by beheading.

Pssst! Scary here...init!

The castle became known as "The Tower"; the tower to be feared.

WOooo

Come 'ere you!

Nobody wanted to be "sent to the Tower!"

Hahaha

I say! One seems to have lost one's head!

When Edward IV died in 1483, his 12 year old son Edward was next in line for the throne. But his uncle, Richard had him and his younger brother lodged in the Tower.

The Duke seized the throne and was crowned King Richard III and soon after the two Princes mysteriously disappeared.

There have been several sightings of a headless figure wandering around the Tower. It is believed to be Anne Boleyn, the second wife of Henry VIII. She was beheaded on Tower Green then buried with her head tucked under her arms.

Give it here! I found it first!

The ghosts of the two Princes have been seen playing around the castle.

Don't read the next page, it's too gory!

Terror-meter

55

Tower of Terror

RANULF FLAMBARD

Seems you were right about the KNOTSsss!

GRUFFYDD AP LLEWELYN

Here are some of the unfortunate inmates of the dreaded Tower of London.

1100 Ranulf Flambard: Bishop of Durham; was the first known prisoner. He was imprisoned by Henry I. But he managed to escape by tying sheets together and climbed out the window.

1241 Gruffydd ap Llewelyn: a Welsh independence fighter. He also tried climbing out the window using sheets, but he didn't tie them very well and fell to his death.

1346 David II: King of Scotland
1356 John II: King of France
1399 Richard II: King of England
1406 James I: King of Scotland
1465 Henry VI: King of England

1546 Anne Askew: the only woman to be tortured at the Tower and was then burned at the stake.

1554 Princess Elizabeth: was only 21 when she was imprisoned here by her half sister Queen Mary.

1605 Guy Fawkes: – was executed in front of the Houses of Parliament for trying to blow them up.

The last beheading in Britain was of Simon Fraser who was executed here in 1747 for his part in the Scottish Battle of Culloden.

The last person to be held prisoner at the Tower was Rudolf Hess in 1941. He was Deputy to Adolf Hitler.

Sir Walter Raleigh was imprisoned here three times. He was eventually beheaded at the Palace of Westminster in 1618.

HERE ARE JUST A FEW OF THE MOST PROMINENT PEOPLE WHO WERE BEHEADED AT THE TOWER. SOME WERE EXECUTED PRIVATELY IN THE TOWER GROUNDS, BUT OTHERS WERE TAKEN TO TOWER HILL, FOR A PUBLIC EXECUTION.

1305. William Wallace, a Scottish independence fighter: beheaded publically on Tower Hill.
1495. Sir William Stanley, Lord Chamberlain to Henry VII: beheaded publically on Tower Hill.
1534. Sir Thomas More, lawyer and social reformer: beheaded publically on Tower Hill.
1541. Margaret Pole, the Countess of Salisbury: beheaded privately at the Tower.
1536. Anne Boleyn, second wife of King Henry VIII: beheaded privately at the Tower.
1540. Thomas Cromwell, lawyer and statesman: beheaded publically on Tower Hill.
1542. Catherine Howard, fifth wife of King Henry VIII: beheaded privately on Tower Green.
1553. Lady Jane Grey: Queen of England for nine days: beheaded privately on Tower Green.

The Show of Heads

The southern Gatehouse on the old London Bridge was the site of the horrific display of severed heads, which were impaled on pikes. This gruesome tradition, usually reserved for traitors, began in 1305, with the head of William Wallace, and continued for 355 years. Heads would be dipped in tar and boiled, to preserve them. It was recorded that, on one day in 1305, there was a total of thirty heads on show.

WARWICK CASTLE 1260

REBUILT IN STONE AROUND 1260, WARWICK CASTLE IS A MASSIVE FORTRESS, RIDDLED WITH TOWERS ALONG ITS HIGH WALLS. BUILT ON A BEND BY THE RIVER AVON, THE CASTLE STANDS OVER THE TOWN OF WARWICK.

A SHORT SIEGE

In 1642, the Earl of Northampton attacked the castle, but he only had two small cannons with him. Although the noise from them **frightened** the people inside, the cannons could not do any damage.

The defenders in the castle had two BIG cannons, and were able to kill quite a few of the attackers. The Earl of Essex soon arrived with his soldiers to help defend the castle. Rather than fight, the Earl of Northampton and his men quickly **ran away**. So, after two weeks, the siege ended.

In the 15th century Richard Neville was the Earl of Warwick and one of the most powerful men in the country. He was known as the 'King Maker'. He actioned the removal of King Henry VI from the throne and installed the new King Edward IV.

The castle has many towers; all with a grim tale to tell!

Take him to **THE TOWER!**

Yes, your Majesty... err... which one?

And what a frightful journey it was too!

The Watergate Tower,
also known as the Ghost Tower, has a resident ghost. In 1628, the owner of the castle, Sir Fulke Greville, was **murdered by his servant** in his London home. Somehow, Sir Fulke's ghost decided to travel to the castle to haunt it.

Bear Tower was where bears were kept to entertain the nobility.

You sure you haven't seen the king?

ACKKK

Caesar's Tower
is the largest. It has a Pit Prison called an "oubliette". A prisoner would be lowered into the small pit, which would then be covered by a metal grill. Quite often the prisoner would be **left there to die.**

But I only came to read the meter!!!

Find out about Siege Machines on page 42

Terror-meter

Royal Windsor

KING HENRY VI

KING H

Here are some of the many Monarchs who lived at Windsor Castle:

King Henry I (reigned 1100–35)
was the first monarch to use it as a palace. He built the first stone Keep.

King Henry II (r.1154–89)
ebuilt the Keep and extended the castle between 1165 and 1179.

King John (r.1199–1216)
used the castle as a base during the revolt of the English Barons.

Edward III (r.1327–77)
created the huge St George's Hall, and founded the "Order of the Garter", the highest order for chivalry.

King Henry V (r.1413–22)
hosted a visit from the Holy Roman Emperor in 1417.

King Henry VI (r. 1422–1461, then 1470–1471)
was born at Windsor and became the youngest ever king when he was just 9 months old. After a quick nappy change, he was ready to rule the country.

King Henry VII (r.1485–1509)
held a huge feast for the Order of the Garter in 1488. This was to become an annual event.

King Henry VIII (r.1509–47)
really enjoyed the Garter Feast and made it a bigger event.

King Edward VI (r.1547–53)
disliked Windsor and stopped the Garter Feasts! Spoilsport!

Queen Elizabeth I (r.1558–1603)
used it for diplomatic engagements. Ten brass cannons were set up to increase its defences.

King James I (r.1603–25)
liked to use Windsor as a base for hunting, but James's English and Scottish followers often quarrelled over rooms.

King Charles I (r.1625–49)
enjoyed the castle ... well, until 1647, when he was held prisoner there by the Roundheads during the English Civil War.

George IV (r.1820–30)
spent a vast amount of money on the castle. He designed the state apartments, added expensive furnishings, and increased the height of the Round Tower.

Queen Victoria (r.1837–1901)
spent most of her time at Windsor, where she often hosted state visits by foreign monarchs.

Queen Elizabeth II decided to use Windsor Castle as a weekend retreat. As an official royal home, she often uses Windsor for state banquets, and for entertaining important visitors from abroad. (r.1952– Long live the Queen!)

KING EDWARD VI

QUEEN ELIZABETH II

KING C

QUEEN

WINDSOR CASTLE 1100

WINDSOR CASTLE IS A GRAND ROYAL PALACE, AND ALSO THE OLDEST AND LARGEST OCCUPIED CASTLE IN THE WORLD. THE ORIGINAL MOTTE AND BAILEY TIMBER CASTLE WAS ONE OF A RING OF NINE CASTLES, BUILT BY WILLIAM THE CONQUEROR TO DEFEND LONDON.

One seems to have lost ones guest...

I'm here!

I've been here for two years.

I'm lost!

HELP!

IT HAS BEEN IMPROVED CONSTANTLY BY ITS ROYAL OWNERS, SINCE KING HENRY I ERECTED THE FIRST STONE CASTLE IN THE 12TH CENTURY.

Ghastly Deeds

King Edward III often used Windsor Castle as a prison. Prisoners were kept in the **Devil's Tower**, or in the dungeons. When executed, their bodies were hung from the Curfew Tower.

You can't beat a good beheading!

Everyone knows hanging is best!

During the **Black Death**, Queen Elizabeth I moved to Windsor. In 1563, she had gallows erected outside the castle, and gave strict orders that anyone coming from London was to be hanged.

Hmmm... beheading? or hanging?

I just can't decide!

The clocks in the Great Kitchen are always five minutes fast, to ensure that the food served to the Queen is never late.

The castle has over 300 fireplaces. I wonder if I could get a job lighting the fires

Terror-meter

61

Ring Of Nine Castles

The Tower of London's awesome White Tower was built after William the Conqueror was crowned King of England in 1066. As London was his main stronghold he built a ring of nine castles to help defend it.

**Berkhamsted   Oxford   Canterbury   Rochester   Guildford
Colchester   Wallingford   Hertford   Windsor**

Can you place the nine castle names into the grid?

WHITE TOWER

YES!
I KNOW I'm
WILLIAM THE
CONQUEROR!
...But this puzzles' really hard.

No Writing on the walls

··Eh! Never Mind!

KING WiLLiE the Silly Billy

MAP

1. ALNWICK
2. ARUNDEL
3. BAMBURGH
4. BEESTON
5. BODIAM
6. CARISBROOKE
7. CARLISLE
8. CLIFFORD'S TOWER
9. CORFE
10. DOVER
11. DUNSTER
12. FRAMLINGHAM
13. KENILWORTH
14. LANCASTER
15. LEEDS
16. LINCOLN
17. PONTEFRACT
18. PORCHESTER
19. ROCHESTER
20. SKIPTON
21. TINTAGEL
22. TOWER OF LONDON
23. WARWICK
24. WINDSOR

HASTINGS

ANSWERS TO PUZZLES

SIEGE THE DIFFERENCE PAGE 43

BEESTON CASTLE PAGE 14
HIDDEN SIX GOLD COINS

1 Up King Richard's sleeve
2 Beside the well
3 Behind mound of earth
4 Beside Captain Steele
5 On entrance to castle
6 Around King Henry's neck

TOWER OF LONDON PAGE 54
HIDDEN SIX RAVENS

1 On the Beefeater
2 Below William the Conqueror
3 Above the castle
4 Below the ghost
5 On the upper castle wall
6 On the axeman

YE OLDE WORDSEARCH PAGE 25

```
N Y J O V M R F B A V C R S F N Y Z
C W V T M Q Y L Z G S T N B V R C H
L O D K C L E R K N C D B Y D X O L
V Z B Q A R F D P T U H L O F U T G
P L N B C O O P E R L Q A W C J T U
H R O P L V Z Y L B I F C V A D A Z
N B C J W E N F C Z I P K G R Z R O
Y D Z A B M R U W T O X S Y P N H T
D C O N S T A B L E N F M B E L X Q
A R B X G V U H Y S L R I S N C B O
Z O Y I N M T A V B Y N T Z T R P Y
M L K U L C R L P E O F H P R U F T
F H Q V R L T G E Z J T W L R H O V
R N C A J P E S M T Y P T D N G L D
T S D P Q B Y R D H C Q M L Y T X N
U C H A N D L E R B O H U K E B H O
P T S V Z Q M S E N F L E G M R Y L
L U C X I Y J F C L T D N R V C E B
```

RING OF NINE CASTLES PAGE 62

```
                    C
      O X F O R D   L
                    C A N T E R B U R Y
W                   H               E
A                   E       H       R
L           W       S       E       K
L           I       T       R       H
I   W H I T E T O W E R     T       A
N           N               F       M
G U I L D F O R D           O       S
F           S               R       T
O   R O C H E S T E R       D       E
R           R                       D
D
```